CLASSIC
Jokes

Compiled and edited by
Jeff Silverman and Lawrence Morgenstern
Illustrated by Dave Cornell

ECW Press

PROPERTY OF
HIGH POINT PUBLIC LIBRARY
HIGH POINT, NORTH CAROLINA

Copyright © Yuk Yuk's Publishing Inc., 2003

Published by ECW Press
2120 Queen Street East, Suite 200, Toronto, Ontario, Canada M4E 1E2

All rights reserved. No part of this publication may be reproduced, stored in a
retrieval system, or transmitted in any form by any process — electronic,
mechanical, photocopying, recording, or otherwise — without the prior written
permission of the copyright owners and ECW Press.

NATIONAL LIBRARY OF CANADA CATALOGUING IN PUBLICATION DATA

Yuk Yuk's joke books

Contents: v. 1. Classic Jokes. — v. 2. Jokes for roasts and toasts.
— v. 3. Jokes men only tell other men.

ISBN 1-55022-606-1 (v. 1.).— ISBN — 1-55022-605-3 (v. 2.).
ISBN 1-55022-607-X (v. 3.).

1. Wit and humor. I. Yuk Yuk's (Toronto, Ont.)

PN6151.Y84 2003   808.87   C2003-902184-X

Cover and Text Design: Tania Craan
Printing: Transcontinental

This book is set in Imago

DISTRIBUTION
CANADA: Jaguar Book Group, 100 Armstrong Avenue, Georgetown, on L7G 5S4

UNITED STATES: Independent Publishers Group, 814 North Franklin Street,
Chicago, Illinois 60610

PRINTED AND BOUND IN CANADA

ECW PRESS
ecwpress.com

Yuk Yuk's "On Tour" offers all types of comedic entertainment for any
occasion. From major concerts to company parties we deliver the laughs.
**Call: Funny Business East: 416-967-6431 Ext. 246
or Funny Business West 403-258-2040.**

PREFACE

They say laughter is the best medicine. Which explains why you need a prescription for nitrous oxide. Everybody, with the exception of Unitarians, loves a good joke. In certain parts of the world, a burp can be taken as either a compliment or an insult, and white, while considered virginal in the West, is feared as the color of motorcycle-riding Demons of Death in Asian countries where opium is legal. What's the point? Just this: no matter where you are on this planet, it's obvious to anyone who sees you laughing that you've found something funny. And that it's probably not Carrot Top.

Humor may depend on cultural mores and historical contexts, but one thing remains constant: the punch line comes at the end of the joke. Or, in the case of a joke written in Hebrew, on the left.

This book, *Yuk Yuk's Joke Book Volume Two: Classic Jokes,* is an assorted collection of jokes in the classic ("old school," if you will) style. The gags contained here are for sharing. Share them with your friends and family members. In fact, feel free to personalize them if doing so will make the joke-telling experience more rewarding. Rephrase them so you are the star of the story. *You* walked into a bar. . . . *You* were two travelling salesmen. . . *You* had a 12-inch pianist. . . .

A brief note on the content of these jokes. As this book goes to press, the prevailing and annoying political correctness movement is still wielding its oppressive might. You may notice a dearth of jokes about citizens of a certain former Soviet Bloc country or certain occupants of a Canadian Maritime province. You know, the one that doesn't like being called a Maritime province. Those jokes are still here; simply substitute whichever racial, sexual, or religious group you'd like when no one is watching.

The 500 jokes in this volume represent all the classic forms of comedy: one-liners, shaggy dog stories, riddles, "How many whatevers does it take to change a lightbulb," and many more. They're all in here for your entertainment. Enjoy.

**He who laughs last. . .
probably didn't get the joke.**

A volunteer was visiting an old lady in a retirement home. As they chatted, he helped himself to some peanuts in a jar on her table. After a while, he asked the old woman if she wanted a peanut. "Oh no, dear," she replied, "I can't chew those things. I just suck the chocolate off them and drop them in the jar."

**There are three kinds of people . . .
those who can count and those who can't.**

**What's the definition of grandparents?
The people who think your children are
wonderful even though they're sure you're
not raising them properly.**

You should always borrow money from
pessimists.
They never expect it back.

**Late one night in Washington, a mugger
jumped in the path of a well-dressed man
and stuck a gun in his ribs.
"Give me your money," he demanded.
Indignant, the man replied, "You can't do
this. I'm a United States congressman."
"In that case," replied the mugger, "give me
my money."**

How many actors does it take to screw in a
lightbulb?
Three. One to change the bulb and the other two
to discuss how they would have done it better.

What do Rubik's Cube and a penis have in common?
The more you play with them, the harder they get.

Always remember, you are a unique, one-of-a-kind individual . . . just like everyone else.

What's the difference between erotic sex and kinky sex?
With erotic sex you use a feather. With kinky sex you use the whole chicken.

Eat right, stay fit . . . die anyway.

You should always go to other people's funerals.
Otherwise, they'll never go to yours.

How do you annoy a mime?
Play a blank tape at full volume.

As long as there are tests . . .
there will always be prayer in school.

How can you tell when a man is well hung?
When you can just barely slip your finger between his neck and the noose.

Always remember that change is inevitable. . .
except from vending machines.

How are husbands like lawnmowers? They're hard to get started, they emit noxious fumes, and they never work half the time.

Why does it take 100 million sperm to fertilize one egg?
Because none of them will stop to ask for directions.

**How many chauvinists does it take to screw in a lightbulb?
None. Let the bitch do the dishes in the dark.**

What does it mean when a man is in your bed gasping for breath and calling your name?
You didn't hold the pillow down long enough.

What goes in dry, comes out wet, and helps you relax?
A tea bag.

One day a famous hypnotist was attempting to break the record for the largest crowd ever to be hypnotized. He assembled 5,000 people in a great auditorium and began waving a watch. "Watch the watch, watch the watch, watch the watch," he chanted over and over. The crowd became mesmerized as the watch swayed back and forth. Thousands of eyes followed the swinging watch, when suddenly the hypnotist's fingers slipped and the watch fell to the floor.

"Shit!" said the hypnotist.

It took three weeks to clean the auditorium.

Sex is like air.
It's no big deal unless you aren't getting any.

Whose cruel idea was it for the word *lisp* to have an *s* in it?

On the first night of their honeymoon, the naive virgin bride slipped into a sexy nightie and crawled into bed only to find her Christian husband on the couch.

"Aren't you going to make love to me?" she asked.

"I can't," he answered.

"Why not?"

"Because it's Lent."

Almost in tears, she yelled, "Well, that's the most ridiculous thing I've ever heard. Who did you lend it and for how long?"

How did the redneck mother teach her son which way to put his underwear on? "Yellow in front, brown in back."

Did you hear about the world's toughest boss? If you were five minutes late, he docked you pay. If you were five minutes early, he charged you rent.

How many teamsters does it take to screw in a lightbulb?
Fifteen. You got a problem with that?

What's the difference between a cheap hooker and an elephant?
One rolls on her back for peanuts, and the other one lives in a zoo.

As the young bride came out of the bathroom in her honeymoon suite, she saw the groom on his knees.

"What are you doing?" she asked.

"I'm praying for guidance," he answered.

"I'll take care of that," she replied. "You pray for endurance."

lightbulb many dyslexics take to does screw a in How it?
.enO

Any time you think no one cares if you're alive or not . . . try missing a couple of car payments.

Just think how deep the ocean would be if sponges didn't live in it.

After eating, do amphibians need to wait an hour before getting out of the water?

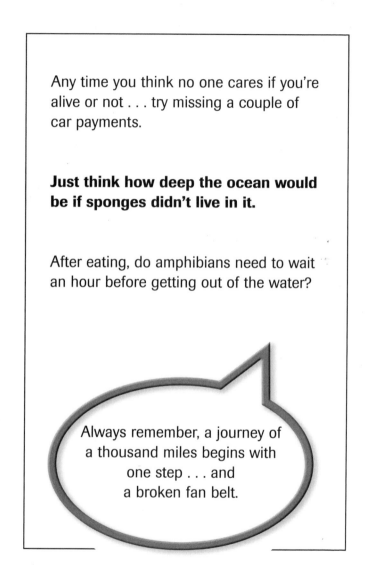

Always remember, a journey of a thousand miles begins with one step . . . and a broken fan belt.

A man is walking in the country when he sees a farmer walking a pig with one of its hind legs missing. "Say, old man," the man asks the farmer, "what happened to your pig's leg?"

"Well, sir," replied the farmer, "this here's just about the smartest pig on Earth. One night about three years ago, a small fire broke out in our kitchen, and this here little pig oinked and jumped around makin' all kinds of commotion till we was all woken up. Saved the whole family. Then about a year ago, I was plowing the north 40 when my tractor flipped over and pinned me underneath. I'd have died if this little pig hadn't run home and alerted my wife. Yes, siree, this is one amazing animal."

"Well, that's an incredible story," said the man, "but what does it have to do with why the pig is missing a leg?"

"Well, hell, it has everything to do with it," replied the farmer. "A pig like that you don't eat all at once."

A man is skydiving for the first time. He pulls on his rip cord, and nothing happens. He pulls his emergency cord, and nothing happens. Just then he sees another person going up. "Hey," he calls to the other guy, "do you know anything about parachutes?"

"No," answers the other guy. "Do you know anything about gas stoves?"

A woman was by her husband's side as he lay on his deathbed. "Darling, come closer, I want to tell you something," he said to her.

She knelt down to hear him.

"My dear Marion, you've been at my side for over 50 years. You stood by me when my first business went bankrupt. When my second business burned to the ground, you were there. You were never out of my sight after I broke my back and was laid up for six months, and you've been with me every day since I was diagnosed with cancer. Marion, my beloved, let's face it . . . you're a goddamned jinx."

What does it mean when a man suggests having dinner by candlelight? There's been a power failure.

Did you hear about the guy who didn't speak to his wife for 18 months? He didn't want to interrupt her.

Bigamy means having one wife too many. According to some, monogamy means the same thing.

What food diminishes a woman's sex drive by 90%? Wedding cake.

Make love, not war . . . or get married and do both.

What's the definition
of amnesia?
The condition that
enables a woman who
has gone through labor
to have sex again.

How many WASPs does it take to screw
in a lightbulb?
Two. One to call the electrician, one to
mix the martinis.

**Why do scientists call it research
when they're looking for something
new?**

Why don't Baptists make love standing up?
It might lead to dancing.

**How many psychiatrists does it take to
screw in a lightbulb?**
**Only one, but the lightbulb has to *want*
to change.**

What's a poor man's Jacuzzi?
Farting in the bathtub.

**Did you hear about the dress code in Las
Vegas?**
You have to wear a tie to lose your shirt.

How many paranoid schizophrenics does
it take to screw in a lightbulb?
Who wants to know?

21

A large dog walks into a butcher shop with a purse in its mouth. He puts the purse down and starts barking.

"What is it, boy?" asks the butcher, smiling. "Do you want to buy some meat?"

The dog barks and nods his head up and down.

Amazed, the butcher asks, "What kind of meat?"

So the dog paws the display case in front of the liver.

Still doubtful, the butcher asks, "How many pounds do you want?"

The dog barks three times.

By now, the butcher is starting to believe the dog is really communicating with him. "Okay," he says. "Three pounds it is. That'll be eight dollars."

The dog picks up the purse and drops it in front of the butcher. The butcher opens it, and sure enough there's exactly eight dollars in it. The butcher is astounded. The dog picks up the purse, puts it in the bag with the liver, takes the bag in his mouth, and leaves. The butcher can't believe it.

He decides to follow the dog. He trails the dog to a house. The dog goes up to the door and scratches on it. The door bursts open, and the man who opened it starts yelling at the dog.

"Stop that," says the butcher. "What are you doing? That's the smartest dog I've ever seen."

"Smart?" counters the man. "This is the fourth time this week he forgot his keys."

Did you hear about the moron who won a gold medal at the Olympics?
He was so proud he had it bronzed.

Did you hear about the redneck who passed away and left his entire estate to his widow? Unfortunately, she couldn't touch it until she turned 14.

How many surrealists does it take to change a lightbulb?
Two. One to hold the giraffe and one to fill the bathtub with brightly colored power tools.

What's the difference between Jewish women and Catholic women?
Catholic women have fake jewelry and real orgasms.

Did you hear about the redneck who was given a toilet brush for his birthday?
He didn't like it, so he went back to using Charmin.

Why are jokes about blondes so short?
So men can remember them.

One day an angel in heaven sees a priest playing golf on Easter. He runs and tells God.

"I'll fix him for this," says God. "Watch this."

Just as the priest hits the ball, God waves his hand, and the ball lands right in the hole. The priest is amazed. As he tees off on the next hole, God waves his hand again, and the tee shot goes right in the hole again. Three more times God does this, until the confused angel asks him, "God, how is this punishing him for playing golf on Easter?"

"Simple," answers God. "Who's he going to tell?"

**How many straight male San Franciscans does it take to screw in a lightbulb?
Both of them.**

Did you hear about the moron who locked his keys in his car?
It took him two hours to get his family out with a coat hanger.

An atheist was fishing in Loch Ness when suddenly the Loch Ness monster attacked his boat. Just as the monster was about to swallow the boat whole, the atheist screamed, "Oh, God, help me!"

At once the monster froze in mid-lunge, and a booming voice called down to the atheist, "I thought you didn't believe in me?"

"Give me a break," the man pleaded. "A minute ago I didn't believe in the Loch Ness monster either."

Did you hear about the restaurant on Mars?
Good food, no atmosphere.

Why did the moron sell his water skis?
He couldn't find a lake with a hill in it.

How can you tell if you have really bad acne?
If it takes a blind man more than an hour to read your face.

A father asked his son about the test he'd had that day at school. "How were the exam questions, boy?"

"They were fine, but I had difficulty with the answers."

What do you call a cow with no legs? Ground beef.

What do a divorce in Alabama, a tornado in Mississippi, and a hurricane in Georgia have in common?
Either way, somebody's bound to lose his trailer.

If you mated a bulldog with a shitsu, would it be called a bullshit?

Can a homeless person be sentenced to house arrest?

How many mystery writers does it take to screw in a lightbulb?
Two. One to screw it in almost all the way and the other to give it a surprising twist at the end.

Health nuts are going to feel pretty stupid one day . . .
lying in the hospital dying of nothing.

Why does a slight tax increase cost you $200 and a substantial tax cut save you 30¢?

How is it that one careless match can start a forest fire, but it takes a whole box to start a barbecue?

How do you know you're really ugly?
You have to trick or treat over the phone.

What do you do when you see an endangered animal eating an endangered plant?

There's a movement in West Virginia to raise the drinking age to 32.
They're trying to get alcohol out of the high schools.

What's the difference between a lightbulb and a pregnant woman? You can unscrew a lightbulb.

What do you call a midget psychic who just escaped from jail?
A small medium at large.

How many men does it take to screw in a lightbulb?
Three. One to screw in the bulb and two to listen to him brag about the screwing part.

What's the difference between a man and a condom?
Condoms have changed. They're no longer thick and insensitive.

What is a man's ultimate embarrassment?
Walking into a wall with an erection and hurting his nose.

Always remember, it's always darkest . . .
before the movie starts.

"I can't find a cause for your illness," the doctor said. "Frankly, I think it's due to drinking."

"In that case," replied his alcoholic patient, "I'll come back later when you're sober."

What's the difference between an oral and a rectal thermometer?
The taste.

You know what's really scary?
You start telling your doctor your symptoms, and he starts backing away.

What do you get when you cross pasta and a boa constrictor?
Spaghetti that winds itself around the fork.

If a parsley farmer is sued, do they garnish his wages?

Why doesn't Mexico have an Olympic team?
Because everyone who can run, jump, and swim
is already in the U.S.

**What's the most outstanding contribution
chemistry has made to society?
Blondes.**

Two men are walking toward each other, each
dragging his left foot. When they meet, one man
points to his leg and says, "Vietnam, 1969."
    The other man points to his leg and says,
"Dog crap, 20 feet back."

**Why did the bird hater buy a bird feeder?
It was cheaper than cat food.**

A jazz musician goes to the doctor for a checkup.

"I'm afraid I have some bad news," the doctor tells him. **"You have only three weeks to live."**

"On what?"

How many brewers does it take to change a lightbulb?
About a third less than it takes to change a regular bulb.

What do you say to an actor with a steady job? "I'll have a burger, large fries, and a coke."

**Where do you find turtles with no legs?
Right where you left them.**

The Concorde travels at twice the speed
of sound . . .
which is great except you can't hear the in-flight
movie until two hours after you land.

A man had no life insurance, but he did have
fire insurance . . .
so his wife had him cremated.

**Quasimodo is in the kitchen when his
mother walks in carrying a wok. "Oh goody,"
he says, "I love Chinese food."**

**His mother says, "What Chinese food?
I'm going to iron your shirts."**

One day the lazy moron's mother told him,
"If you procrastinate, you'll never amount to
anything."
To which he replied, "Oh yeah? Just you wait."

A poor immigrant comes to America because he heard that the streets were paved with gold. As soon as he leaves the airport main entrance, he looks down and sees a gold bracelet covered in diamonds. He bends down to pick it up and then stops. "What the hell," he says, "I'll start on Monday."

A skeleton walks into a bar and says, "Hey, bartender. I'll have a beer and a mop."

How do we know the toothbrush was invented by a redneck?
Anyone else would have called it a "teethbrush."

A Chinese newlywed couple are on their honeymoon when the groom tells his young bride, "I want to try 69."

She replies, "You want beef with broccoli?"

What do little birdies see when they get knocked unconscious?

A guy goes into his analyst's office and complains, "Everyone's always rushing me." The analyst says, "Your hour's up."

A priest was delivering a eulogy for a member of his congregation. "Walter was always known for his words of encouragement and inspiration," said the priest. "In fact, just minutes before he died in the hospital, too incapacitated to speak, he handed me a note. I folded it up and put it in my pocket. I haven't had a chance to read it until now. I'm sure it will comfort us all." The priest unfolded the note and read it. "You're standing on my oxygen hose."

Why is a barbed wire fence like a bikini? It protects the property but doesn't obstruct the view.

During a course in human sexuality, the teacher was discussing items in the Kinsey report. The students gasped when the teacher read about a woman who'd had several hundred orgasms in a single session.

"Wow," said a male student, "who was she?"

To which a female student responded, "To hell with that, who was _he_?"

How do you know you're really ugly?
You sign up for an ugly contest, and they say, "Sorry, no professionals."

A ship carrying red paint collided with a ship carrying purple paint.
Both crews were marooned.

"I just finished a speed-reading course and read _War and Peace_ in under an hour," the proud moron told his buddy.

"What was it about?" his friend asked him.

"Something about Russia."

The best way to die
is peacefully in
your sleep . . .
not screaming like the
passengers in your car.

Why did the ape read the Bible and Darwin's *Origin of Species*? He wanted to know if he was his brother's keeper or his keeper's brother.

New-car prices are so high one dealer now has a show room . . . and a recovery room.

An Irishman is walking along the beach one day, and he sees a bottle lying on the sand. He picks it up, brushes it off, and out pops a genie.

The genie says, "Since you have freed me from the bottle, I will grant you three wishes."

The Irishman thinks for a minute and says, "I'm a might thirsty. I think I'll be wishing for a pint of stout."

POOF! There is a pint of stout in his hand. The Irishman drinks it down and starts to throw the bottle away.

"I'd look at that bottle again before I threw it away if I were you. This is a magic bottle that will fill back up every time you empty it. Now, what are your other wishes?"

The Irishman looks at the bottle and says, "I believe I'll have two more of these."

How do you know you're getting fat?
You get up to dance at a nightclub, and the live band skips.

An old man is driving down the highway when his cell phone rings. It's his wife, and she's very worried. "Honey, be careful," she tells him. "I just heard on the news there's an idiot driving the wrong way on the interstate."

"Hell," says the old man. "It's not just one car. There are hundreds of them."

Did you hear about the moron who was thrilled that he finished a jigsaw puzzle in 87 days?
On the box it said three to five years.

Two morons walk into a bar eating sandwiches.

The bartender looks at them and says, "Hey, you guys can't eat your own food in here."

So they swap sandwiches.

What happens when you play a country song backward? You reconcile with your wife, your runaway dog returns home, and your overturned pick-up rolls back on its wheels.

Two men are fishing at a riverbank when a funeral procession drives by. One of the men stands up, takes off his hat, holds it over his heart, and bows.

"That was a nice thing to do," the other man tells him.

"Well, we were married for 25 years."

A teacher was wrapping up class and reminded everyone about the big test the next day. "Now remember, barring a medical emergency or a death in the family, there will be no excuse for missing tomorrow's exam."

One smart-ass student yelled out, "What about sexual exhaustion?"

After the laughter died down, the teacher shot back, "You can still write with the other hand."

A drunk gets on the bus late one night after tying one on and sits next to an elderly woman. She looks the man up and down and says, "I've got news for you. You're going straight to hell."

The man jumps out of his seat and shouts, "Good heavens, I'm on the wrong bus."

How do you know you're getting fat?
When you go to the movies, not only do you need two seats, but also you can't feel the armrest in the middle.

Why didn't the dumb lady change the baby's diaper for a month?
Because it said right on the package "Good for up to 20 pounds."

A guy tries to get into a nightclub, but the doorman tells him there's a dress code, and he has to wear a tie. So the guy goes to his car and looks for anything he can use as a tie. All he can find is a pair of jumper cables. So he puts them around his neck, goes back to the club, and asks the doorman if he can get in now. The doorman says, "All right. . . . But don't you start anything."

Did you hear about the considerate husband? He didn't like to hear his wife struggle with housework . . .
so he turned up the volume on the TV.

Why is Christmas just like a day at the office? Because you do all the work, and the fat guy with the suit gets all the credit.

A little boy came home from his first day at school and asked his mother, "Mommy, what's sex?"

His mother, who was a little embarrassed, spent the next 10 minutes explaining the subject as intelligently and delicately as she could.

When she finished, the little boy pulled out his enrollment form from school and said, "How am I going to get all that onto this one little square?"

What do you get when you cross a turkey with a porcupine?
A Thanksgiving dinner you can eat and pick your teeth with at the same time.

Did you hear about the shy, retiring bookkeeper? He was shy about 20 grand. That's why he's retiring.

How many Deadheads does it take to screw in a lightbulb?
None. They all just wait for it to burn out . . . and then follow it around for 20 years.

Two cannibals are eating a clown. One turns to the other one and says, "Does this taste funny to you?"

A guy goes to the vet and says, "My goldfish has rheumatism."
The vet says, "Keep him out of damp places."

What's the definition of an ecologist?
That's a guy who writes a 600-page book asking where all the trees have gone.

Did you hear about the book on the government's plan to lower taxes?
It's in the fiction section.

How can a woman find out what life is like without a man around?
Get married.

Did you hear about the Siamese twins who moved to England?
The other one wanted to drive.

Did you hear about the organization that fights inflation?
It raised its dues and lost all its members.

What do you call a musician without a girlfriend?
Homeless.

What has four legs and one arm?
A pitbull.

**What's the definition of a schmuck?
Someone who lends a friend $9,000 for
plastic surgery and then can't recognize
the guy to get his money back.**

How do you know you're getting fat?
You drive over a speed bump and smooth it out.

What do you send to a sick florist?

How can you tell if you have really bad breath?
When you talk, people duck.

**How do you know if you were an unwanted
child?
When your parents sent you out on
Halloween, they dressed you up as a parking
space.**

The hunter told his friend that he'd had to shoot his dog.

"Was he mad?" asked his friend.

"He certainly wasn't happy."

How do you know when you have a hygiene problem?
Your teeth are so yellow that every time you smile traffic slows down.

Did you hear about the two seagulls that were flying over the Kentucky Derby?
The first one said, "I'm gonna put everything I got on number seven."

A cement mixer collided with a prison van. Motorists were asked to be on the lookout for 16 hardened criminals.

How do you know you're old?
You have a picture of Moses in your yearbook.

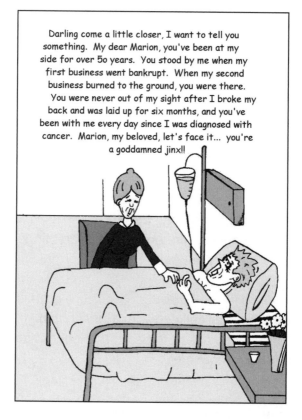

How do you know you're getting fat? You break your leg, and it bleeds gravy.

A professor was giving a big test to his students one day. Once the test was over, the students all handed it back in. The professor noticed that one of the students had stapled a $100 bill to his test with a note that read "A dollar a point." The next day, the professor handed out the results, and the student who'd tried to bribe him got back his test and $64 in change.

A woman visits her son in a far-off college town. Having never visited him before, she's a little shocked when she knocks on his apartment door and a young girl answers.

"Hi, Mom," says her son from inside the apartment. "This is Jenny. She's my roommate. I need help with the rent."

"I see," says the woman. "And nothing's going on?"

"Of course not, Mom. We're just friends."

The woman doesn't say any more on the subject, and a week later she goes back home. A few days later, when the young man comes home, the girl is waiting for him a little upset.

"I don't want to cast aspersions on your mother, but my fancy silver soup ladle is missing. The last time I saw it was the day before she arrived."

The son doesn't know what to do. He e-mails his mother and broaches the subject as delicately as he can. "Dear Mother: I'm not saying you 'did' take Jenny's silver ladle, and I'm not saying you 'didn't' take it. But the fact remains that it's missing since you visited us."

His mother e-mailed back, "Dear Son: I'm not saying that you 'are' sleeping with Jenny, and I'm not saying you 'are not' sleeping with her. But the fact of the matter is, if she were sleeping in her own bed, she would have found the ladle by now."

How do you know when you're really ugly? You walk through the airport, and even the Hare Krishnas avoid you.

How do you know you're really fat?
You walk into a restaurant wearing corduroys, and they put you in the smoking section.

How do you know when you've got bad dandruff? You lean over an aquarium, and the fish think it's feeding time.

What's the definition of bad business instincts? Outbidding everyone for the Father's Day card concession at a home for unwed mothers.

What's the worst thing about cigarettes in the urinals?
It makes them soggy and hard to light.

How do you know when it's time to junk your car?
When its bluebook price doubles every time you fill up the tank.

When it comes to efficiency, you just can't beat the mob.
Who else sends out get well cards two days before the accident?

A guy says to his boss, "I'd like to take the day off to attend my mother-in-law's funeral."
The boss says, "Who wouldn't?"

What's the number one rule for plumbers?
Whatever you do, don't bite your fingernails.

**What's the definition of a shotgun wedding?
A case of wife or death.**

Did you hear about the moron hit-man who was
sent to blow up a mob informant's car?
He burned his lips on the tailpipe.

**Did you hear about the pessimist's medic
alert bracelet?
It reads "In case of an accident . . . I'm not
surprised."**

Always remember, you can pick your friends, and
you can pick your nose . . .
but you can't wipe your friends on the couch.

**Your bathroom mirror fogs up, and you
haven't turned on the shower yet.**

As the moron was leaving the hotel, the doorman stuck his hand out and said, "I hope you won't forget me, sir."

And he didn't. He wrote to him every week.

How do you know you're really a wreck? You need two shots of bourbon to calm down enough so you can open the bottle of Valium.

How many successful jumps do you need to join the skydivers' association? All of them.

A college professor in an anatomy class asked his students to sketch a naked man. As he walked around the classroom checking the sketches, he noticed that a sexy young co-ed had sketched a man with an erection.

The professor commented, "No, no, I wanted it the other way."

The sexy co-ed replied, "What other way?"

Did you hear about the moron whose uncle's funeral got more and more expensive every day?
He'd buried him in a rented tux.

The moron bought a talking car, but it turns out he got conned.
The salesman was a ventriloquist.

Why should you always travel with a six pack in the winter?
In case you have to leave a message in the snow.

Did you hear about the guy who figured out
a way to beat parking tickets?
He removed his windshield wipers.

**Parents have to learn to see the best in
things. For example, if your daughter comes
home from college with a little bundle in her
arms . . .**
be glad it's just laundry.

How do you know you're really ugly?
You get abducted, and the kidnappers put
blindfolds over their eyes.

**How do you know when you're getting fat?
Your driver's license photo says "To be
continued."**

There's a new book on the market entitled *How to Be Happy without Money*. It costs $45.

What do you get when your mother-in-law drives off a cliff in your brand-new Mercedes? Mixed emotions.

What do a man and a dog have in common?
They're both afraid of the vacuum.

What do you get when you cross an elephant with a rich woman?
The world's most expensive nose job.

A guy goes to the dentist and says, "Doc, you gotta help me. My gums are shrinking." The dentist says, "Idiot! You're brushing your teeth with Preparation H."

A Jew and a Chinese guy are drinking in a bar when suddenly the Jew throws his drink in the Chinese guy's face.

"What was that for?" he asks the Jew.

"That was for Pearl Harbor."

"Pearl Harbor? That wasn't us. That was the Japanese."

"Chinese, Japanese, Taiwanese. What difference does it make? You're all the same."

So they go back to drinking, and the Chinese guy throws his drink in the Jew's face.

"What was that for?" asks the Jew.

"That was for the *Titanic*."

"*Titanic*? That wasn't us. That was an iceberg."

"Iceberg, Goldberg, Steinberg. What difference does it make? You're all the same."

How do you know you're an unwanted child? Your only bath toys are a radio and a toaster.

What's an innuendo?
An Italian suppository.

What kind of shampoo do Siamese twins use?
Extra body.

How do you know you have a hygiene problem?
You're missing so many teeth that it looks like your tongue is in jail.

How do you know you're getting old?
You worry about losing your memory but can't remember why.

How do you know you have a bad dentist?
You ask him what to do about yellow teeth, and he tells you to wear a brown tie.

A diner asked the waitress for meatloaf and some kind words. She brought the meatloaf but didn't say a thing.

"Hey, where are the kind words?" he asked.
"Don't eat the meatloaf."

A drunk stumbles into a confessional. The priest hears him come in, but then hears nothing else, so he knocks on the wall. The drunk mumbles, "Forget it, buddy. There's no paper in here either."

How do you know your psychic is a fake?
She talks to you for half an hour and still hasn't sensed that you're not going to pay.

**Did you hear about the jail for morons?
No locks, no bars . . .
just a sign that reads "Simon says stay."**

**Did you hear about the guy who loved
crossword puzzles?
When he died, they buried him six down
and three across.**

How do you know if you're really ugly?
Your father takes you to work every day so he
doesn't have to kiss you good-bye.

**Did you hear about the obese guy arrested
at the border for smuggling drugs?
They looked in his pants and found
a hundred pounds of crack.**

The great thing about advertising is that it brings
quick results. One company advertised that it
needed a new security guard, and the very next
day . . .
it was robbed.

**Why do rednecks go to family reunions?
To meet women.**

Two dwarfs pick up two prostitutes and take them to a hotel. The first dwarf is unable to achieve an erection, and he becomes even more depressed when, for hours, all he can hear from his buddy's room next door is "one, two, three . . . ugh!"

The next morning they're having breakfast when the second dwarf asks, "So how did it go last night?"

"It was so embarrassing. I couldn't get it up."

The second dwarf shook his head. "You think that's bad? I couldn't even get on the bed all goddamn night."

Did you hear about the Chinese diet?
You can eat all you want, but you can use
only one chopstick.

How can you tell you're getting fat?
Your Chapstick is in an aerosol can.

**What's a redneck's idea of safe sex?
When no other cars are coming.**

Did you hear about the moron who saw the antidrug ad that read "Say NO to crack"?
He immediately pulled up his jeans.

**What do you get when you cross a carrier pigeon with a woodpecker?
A bird that not only delivers messages to its destination but also knocks on the door when it gets there.**

If two rednecks get divorced . . .
are they still brother and sister?

Nobody pays attention to the speed limit. The only people who drive 55 miles an hour . . . are parking attendants.

Girls are wearing less and less on the beach these days.
Which is perfect for old men whose memory is starting to go.

Did you hear about the guy whose gambling brought his family together? He lost all his money, and they all had to move into one room.

Did you hear about the new diet? You eat Limburger cheese, garlic, and onions. From a distance, you look thinner.

A moron calls the fire department and says, "Help! My house is on fire."
The fireman asks, "How do we get there?"
"What happened to your red truck?"

How do you spot a redneck during Christmas?
He goes gift shopping for his mom, sister, and wife . . .
and only has to get one present.

An Englishman, an Irishman, and a Scotsman are having a drink in a bar. The Englishman says, "I think my wife is having an affair. The other day I came home and found wire cutters under the bed, and they weren't mine."

The Scotsman says, "I think my wife is having

an affair with a plumber. I came home yesterday and found a pipe wrench under the bed that wasn't mine."

The Irishman says, "I think my wife is having an affair with a horse."

The other two look at him. "A horse?"

"Yes, a horse," says the Irishman. "I came home and found a jockey under the bed."

What's the difference between a drunk and an alcoholic?
A drunk doesn't have to go to those meetings.

If you laid every cigarette smoker end to end around the world . . .
67% of them would drown.

How do you know you're in a tough neighborhood?
People don't ask you for the time; they just take your watch.

A guy at the airport goes up to the ticket desk with three suitcases. He says to the woman behind the counter, "I want this suitcase to go to Toronto. Send this suitcase to Chicago and this one to L.A."

The woman tells him, "I'm sorry, sir, we can't do that."

"Why not? You did it last week."

What's the definition of sheer panic?
Being stuck in traffic after you've had two cups of coffee and a bran muffin.

Did you hear about the drunk who read about the dangers of drinking?
He gave up reading.

Did you hear about the asthmatic girl who got an obscene phone call?
After five minutes, the guy asked, "Did I call you, or did you call me?"

How do you know if your teacher is hung over?
She makes your class take a nap at nine o'clock in the morning . . .
and you're in high school.

How do you know when you have a real drinking problem?
You use a bar stool as a walker to get home.

How do you know if you're an unwanted child?
Your mother lets you lick the beaters on her mixer, but she doesn't turn it off.

How do you know if you're an unwanted child? Your earliest childhood memory is of walking home from the hospital.

How do you know you're really fat? Your proctologist quits because he's afraid of the dark.

Did you hear about the nearsighted whale that fell in love with a submarine?
Every time the submarine shot off a torpedo, it passed out cigars.

A Scotsman in a kilt got drunk and passed out in a ditch. As he slept, two schoolgirls walked by and saw him. They decided to play a joke on him, so one of the girls took the blue ribbon from her hair and tied it to his manhood, and off they went giggling at their prank. After a while, the Scotsman woke up, and as he went to relieve himself he noticed the blue ribbon. After several moments of bewilderment, he said, "I don't know where you've been laddie, but it's nice to know you won first prize."

How do you know you're really fat?
You go to the ball game, and the vendors flip a coin to see who gets your section.

How do you know when you're ugly?
They move the date of Halloween to coincide with your birthday.

How do you know when you're getting old?
When you realize that you can get along without sex but not your glasses.

How do you know if you're an unwanted child?
You ask your dad to play tag, and he says, "Okay, I'll drive."

How do you know you're really ugly?
Your mom had to get drunk to breast-feed you.

Why don't rednecks like edible underwear?
Because, after you wear them for a couple of weeks, they taste the same as the regular ones.

What's the definition of agony?
A one-armed man hanging off a cliff with a wicked case of jock itch.

How do you know when you're really ugly?
You walk into a bank, and they turn off the surveillance cameras.

Why do giraffes have such long necks?
Because their feet stink.

What do you call a reformed drunk who works at
an upholstery shop?
A recovering alcoholic.

A guy goes to the optometrist. He opens the
door and says to the receptionist, "I think I
need my eyes checked."
She says, "You're not kidding. This is the
ladies' room."

What's your first clue you're an unwanted child?
You're baptized in boiling water.

How can you spot a moron at a
cockfight?
He's the one with the duck.

An old woman is riding in an elevator. It stops, and two very rich women get on smelling of expensive perfume.

The first one looks at the old woman arrogantly and says, "Romance by Ralph Lauren—$150 an ounce."

The second one, not to be outdone, sniffs, "Chanel No. 5—$200 an ounce."

After a few moments, the elevator stops at the old woman's floor, and the doors open. As the old woman leaves, she turns to the other two, lets loose with a huge fart, and says, "Broccoli—49¢ a pound."

What did the leper say at the fancy restaurant?
"Could I have another finger bowl, please? Mine is full."

Did you hear about the girl who was half Irish and half Italian?
She mashed potatoes with her feet.

What's the difference between a pitbull and a woman with PMS?
Lipstick.

There's a new aftershave coming out that's made from cow manure. One sniff and women are on you like flies.

What's the difference between outlaws and in-laws?
Outlaws are wanted.

A wealthy benefactor was visiting the local hospital when, during her tour of the floors, she passed a room where a male patient was masturbating.

"Oh, my goodness!" said the lady. "That's disgraceful. Why is he doing that?"

The doctor leading the tour explained, "That man has a very serious condition where the testicles rapidly fill with semen. If he doesn't do that five times a day, they'll explode, and he'll die within minutes."

"Oh my, that's awful," said the lady.

In the next room was a female nurse performing oral sex on a different male patient.

"Oh, my God!" said the lady. "Now how do you justify that?"

The doctor replied, "Same illness, better health plan."

Did you hear about the guy with the really bad case of hiccups?
He sat down on the toilet and siphoned the bowl dry.

How do you know you're getting really fat?
Your ass is so low that every time you fart you
blow sand in your shoes.

**What's a good indication that you should
be on a diet?
Your wedding portrait is a mural.**

An old guy goes to the doctor. The doctor tells
him, "You've got cancer and Alzheimer's."
The old guy says, "At least I don't have cancer."

**A girl goes up to a guy in a bar and says,
"I'll do anything for a hundred dollars."
The guy says, "Great. Paint my house."**

Did you hear about the new dog breed that's
half pitbull and half collie?
After it mauls you, it goes for help.

Have you heard about the new welfare doll? You wind it up, and it doesn't work.

How do we know life isn't fair?
If it was, Elvis would be alive, and all the impersonators would be dead.

How do you know you've got a dirty house?
You have to go outside to wipe your feet.

A man is walking in the countryside when he sees a redneck farmer standing by his fence with a dog, a horse, and a sheep. An accomplished ventriloquist, the man decides to play a joke on the farmer. "Hello there," he says. "That's a nice-looking dog you have. Mind if I talk to it?"

"The dog don't talk," says the farmer.

The man leans down and says to the dog, "Hello, boy. How do you like living with your master?"

To the farmer's amazement, the dog begins to talk. "Oh, I like it just fine," the dog "answers." "My master feeds me great food and plays fetch with me all the time."

The man then asks the farmer, "Can I talk to your horse?"

"The horse don't talk," answers the farmer.

"How do you like your master?" the man asks the horse.

"I like him even more than the dog does," "answers" the horse. "He treats me wonderfully. He feeds me the best oats, brushes my coat every day, and lets me run around the whole farm."

The farmer is amazed.

The man asks, "Can I talk to your sheep?"

The farmer replies nervously, "The sheep's a liar."

A man leaned toward an attractive woman at a bar and said, "Haven't I seen you somewhere before?"
"Yes," she answered. "I'm the receptionist at the VD clinic."

How do you know you're fat?
You have to iron your pants in the driveway.

What do you get when you cross a cow with a giraffe?
A guernsey you need a ladder to milk.

Did you hear about the suicidal dyslexic?
He kept throwing himself *behind* a moving bus.

**Why did the blind woman never change
her baby's diaper?
So she could find him.**

How long has it been since rednecks have
watched the Oscars?
Since *Smokey and the Bandit* was snubbed for
Best Picture.

**When do you know it's time to improve your
personal hygiene?
You blow someone a kiss, and she gets a
canker sore.**

How do you get 20 executives in a minivan?
Promote one and watch the other 19 crawl up
his ass.

What do you call a dog with three legs? Tippy.

Why don't Jehovah's Witnesses like Halloween?
Too many bizarre-looking strangers knock on their doors and annoy them.

Did you hear about the lonely guy who called one of those phone sex lines?
He got a girl who stuttered, and it cost him $1,500.

What has 200 legs and 42 teeth?
A redneck marching band.

Did you hear about the little boy and girl who got caught playing doctor? Fortunately, it was Wednesday, and they were just playing golf.

Have you ever noticed that everyone who drives slower than you is an idiot?
And every one who drives faster is a maniac.

A 12-year-old boy walks into a bar and orders a beer. The waitress looks at him and says, "Kid, do you want to get me in trouble?"

The kid says, "Maybe after the beer."

What's the definition of endless love?
Two blind guys playing tennis.

A young executive was leaving the office late one night when he saw the company's CEO standing in front of the paper shredder. The CEO looked at him with a worried look and said, "Can you help me out here? This is a very sensitive and important document. My secretary usually deals with this, but she left for the day. I wonder if you know how to work this thing."

"Sure I do," said the young executive. He took the paper, put it in the shredder, and turned it on.

"Thanks a lot," said the CEO. "I need two copies."

What's the difference between a drummer and Dr. Scholl's foot pads?
Dr. Scholl's foot pads buck up the feet.

Did you hear about the guy who got fired from his job at the orange juice factory?
He couldn't concentrate.

A customer at a bank asked the loan officer, "How do I stand on getting a $10,000 loan?" The loan officer told him, "You don't stand— you grovel."

What do you call an Amish guy with his arm up a horse's ass?
A mechanic.

**Did you hear about the guy who quit his job at the pool maintenance company?
It was just too draining.**

Did you hear about the moron loan shark?
He lent out all his money and then skipped town.

**How does a union fairy tale begin?
Once upon a time and a half.**

What did the cannibals give the cannibal who was late for dinner?
The cold shoulder.

If a dog is happy, he'll wag his tail. What will a goose do?
Make him growl.

How did the blind woman pierce her ears?
Answering the staple gun.

Why did the company hire a psychiatrist and a proctologist?
To fix their odds and ends.

What do fat people do in the summer?
Stink.

A priest, a minister, and a rabbi are standing in a field. The priest says, "Let's draw a circle and throw our money in the air. Whatever lands outside the circle we keep; whatever lands in the circle we give to God."

The minister says, "I have a better idea. We keep only whatever lands *inside* the circle."

The rabbi says, "How about this? We throw the money in the air. Whatever God wants he can keep."

How do you know if your farts are bad?
The National Weather Service names them.

A blind guy goes into a china shop, picks his dog up by the tail, and starts spinning it around. The clerk says, "May I help you?"
The blind guy answers, "No thanks, I'm just browsing."

What should you do when a musician comes to your door?
Pay him and take your pizza.

Why is a boss like a diaper?
He's always on your ass, and he's usually full of crap.

Why don't morons eat pickles?
Because they can't get their heads in the jar.

What do you give an elephant with diarrhea?
Lots of room.

One cannibal turns to the other cannibal and says, "Your wife makes some really good soup."
**   The other cannibal says, "I don't know. She tastes a little salty to me."**

A guy says to the salesgirl, "I want to buy some toilet paper."

The salesgirl asks him, "What color?"

"Just give me the white paper; I'll color it myself."

Why did the redneck walk his son to school every day?
Because they were both in the same grade.

Did you hear about the gay mafia?
If they get mad at you, they break the legs on your coffee table.

Experts have announced the development of a new fuel made from male brain tissue. It's called assohol.

What's a premature ejaculator's favorite time to make love?
Daylight saving time.

How can you tell if a proctologist is having
a bad day?
His thermometer is behind his ear, and he's
looking for his pencil.

How does a rich snob propose marriage?
"Darling, how would you like to be buried
with my people?"

What do you call a French janitor at Seaworld?
Jacques Custodian.

How come more people don't go elephant
hunting?
It's too tiring to carry the decoys.

Did you hear about the morons who formed
a car pool?
They met at work.

What did the cat say after eating the canary?
"This should put a feather in my crap."

Why do fathers advise their sons to aim high?
So they won't splash on their shoes.

If a boxer wears boxer shorts and a jockey wears jockey shorts, what do you call a guy who doesn't wear any shorts?
A swinger.

How can you tell if the mob is at the cockfight?
The duck wins.

One day the pope was doing a crossword puzzle when he was stumped by one particular word. He turned to one of his cardinals and asked, "Do you know a four-letter word for woman ending in U-N-T?"

The cardinal was a bit flustered but then regained his composure. "Why, 'aunt,' your holiness," he replied.

"Oh yes, of course," said the pope. "Er . . . do you have an eraser?"

How did the mathematician cure his constipation?
He worked it out with a pencil.

How do you know if you're really ugly?
The local peeping Tom asks you to keep your shades down.

You can't take it with you.
If you could, there'd be a U-Haul behind every hearse.

If Moses were alive today, he'd come down from Mount Sinai with the Ten Commandments . . .
and spend the next five years trying to get them published.

A man walks into a bar in Alabama and orders a grape juice.

The bartender eyes him suspiciously. "You ain't from around here, are ya, boy?" he says.

"No," says the man. "I'm from Pennsylvania."

"What do you do in Pennsylvanee?" asks the bartender.

"I'm a taxidermist," replies the man.

"What the hell is that?"

The man says, "I mount dead animals."

The bartender turns to the others in the bar and shouts, "It's okay, boys. He's one of us."

What do you call a missionary who's been shot full of arrows?
Holier than thou.

Three nuns die in a car crash. They are standing at the pearly gates when Saint Peter greets them. "Before I let you into heaven, you all have to answer one question," says Saint Peter.

The first nun steps forward. "I am ready for my question," she says.

"Who was the first man on Earth?" asks Saint Peter.

"Adam," answers the first nun.

"You are correct," says Saint Peter. "You may enter heaven."

Suddenly, lights flash, bells toll, and the gates swing open. The first nun goes through.

"I am ready for my question," says the second nun.

"Who was the first woman?" asks Saint Peter.

"Eve," answers the second nun.

"That's right," says Saint Peter.

Suddenly, lights flash, bells toll, and the gates swing open.

"You may enter heaven," says Saint Peter.

He then looks at the third nun. "Here is your question. What was the first thing Eve said to Adam?"

The third nun thinks for a moment. "My goodness, that's a hard one," she says.

Suddenly, lights flash, bells toll, and the gates swing open.

Prosperity is having Twinkies after every meal. A recession is having Twinkies after every other meal. A depression is when Twinkies are the meal.

Thomas Edison said that genius is one percent inspiration and 99% perspiration.
Can you imagine anyone that sweaty handling electricity?

Beverly Hills is a very rich community.
The unemployment office has valet parking.

Did you hear about the really small town?
They had to close the zoo when the cat died.

114

What does a farmer call constipation?
Crap failure.

**How do you know when you've let loose with an incredible fart?
Your girlfriend calls you collect and tells you you're disgusting.**

How many Christians does it take to change a lightbulb?
None. They wait for three days, and it comes back on itself.

**How do you know when you're really ugly?
Cops pull you over and order you to speed up.**

There are two nude statues, one male, one female, standing across from each other in a little park. One day an angel comes down from heaven, and with a wave of his hand the two statues are brought to life. "I have been sent to make you both human after so many years of standing across from each other, unable to move. You may do whatever you want to do, but you must hurry, for you can remain alive for only 15 minutes."

The two statues look at each other and start giggling. They take each other's hand and rush into the bushes. After a short while, they emerge.

The angel smiles at them. "That was only seven minutes. Why don't you go back and do it again?"

The statues look at each other, and the female statue says, "Why not? But let's reverse it. This time you hold the pigeon down, and I'll crap on it."

Two old ladies are having a smoke outside their nursing home when it starts to rain. One of the old ladies pulls out a condom and puts it on the cigarette.

The other old lady asks her, "What's that?"

The first old lady tells her, "It's a condom. It keeps my cigarette dry. You can get them at the drugstore."

So the second old lady goes to the drugstore and asks the clerk for a box of condoms. Somewhat flustered by an elderly woman asking for prophylactics, the clerk shyly asks her, "What kind would you like, ma'am?"

"It doesn't matter, sonny. As long as it fits a Camel."

A businessman came home from work one day all depressed. His wife asked him what was wrong.

"You know those aptitude tests we're giving at the office?" he asked. "Well, I took one today, and it's a good thing I own the company."

Heaven is a place where . . .
the lovers are Italian,
the cooks are French,
the mechanics are German,
the police are English, and
the government is run by the Swiss.

Hell is a place where . . .
the lovers are Swiss,
the cooks are English,
the mechanics are French,
the police are German, and
the government is run by the Italians.

Where does virgin wool come from?
Ugly sheep.

What do you do with an elephant with
three balls?
Walk him and pitch to the rhino.

A lady goes to the dentist, and he tells her, "I'm going to have to pull one of your teeth."

The lady says, "I'd rather have a baby than get a tooth pulled."

The dentist says, "Well, make up your mind. I need to know how to adjust the chair."

Why do rednecks have such beautiful noses?
They're all hand-picked.

What's the stuff between an African elephant's toes?
Slow natives.

How do you get a one-armed moron out of a tree?
Wave at him.

Why don't they make mouse-flavored cat food?

A man says to his wife, "How come you never tell me when you have an orgasm?"
"Because you're never around."

What's the difference between men and government bonds?
The bonds will mature one day.

A man asks his wife, "Hey, honey, you want to switch positions tonight?"
"Sure," she answers. "You do the ironing while I sit on the couch and fart."

A man says to his wife, "What the hell do you do with all the grocery money I give you?"
She says, "Look in the mirror and turn sideways."

What do you call a woman who knows where her husband is every night?
A widow.

Three men died and went to heaven. Saint Peter met them at the pearly gates and asked them if they'd been faithful to their wives.

"I cheated on my wife twice," said the first man.

Saint Peter told him that he was forgiven and that he would receive a car to drive in heaven, but it would only be a compact car.

The second man admitted to cheating on his wife once.

Saint Peter told him that he was forgiven and that he would be given a car also. Since he'd cheated once, he got a midsize car.

The third man proudly announced that he'd never cheated on his wife.

"Commendable," said Saint Peter. "For being loyal, you get to drive a luxury car."

A little while later, all three were stopped at a red light. The first two men noticed the third man was upset. They asked him what could possibly be wrong. After all, he had a luxury car.

"I just passed my wife," he told them, "and she was on a skateboard."

Why are married women heavier than single women?
Single women go home, see what's in the fridge, and go to bed. Married women go home, see what's in bed, and go to the fridge.

Why did God make women so beautiful?
So men would love them.
Why did God make women so dumb?
So they would love men.

A woman walks into the kitchen to find her husband swatting flies. "Have you killed any yet, oh great hunter?" she says with a grin. "Sure have," he says. "Five so far. Three male and two female."
"How do you know that?" she asks.
"Simple," he replies. "Three were on a beer can and two on the phone."

Why do rednecks
prefer clear garbage bags?
It makes it easier to go
window shopping.

Did you hear about the moron who read
that 90% of all accidents happen close to
home?
So he moved.

**Why did the pervert cross the road?
He was looking for a chicken.**

What do you get when you cross a
Jehovah's Witness with an atheist?
A guy who knocks on your door for no
reason.

A rabbit and a snake, both blind from birth, meet in the forest one day. They get to talking, and the rabbit asks the snake, "Could you do me a favor? Being blind from birth, I don't know what kind of animal I am. Could you feel my body and tell me what I am?"

So the snake wraps himself around the rabbit. "You're kind of warm with real soft fur and long furry ears."

"I must be a bunny," says the rabbit.

"Now that I did that for you, could you return the favor?" asks the snake.

"Sure," replies the rabbit. So he runs his paws all over the snake. "Hmm, this is strange. You're kind of cold and slimy, and for the life of me I can't tell your head from your ass."

"Gee," says the snake. "I must be an agent."

The greatest salesman in the world is the one who sold two milking machines to a farmer with just one cow . . .
and then took the cow as a down payment.

What's the secret of eternal youth?
Lie about your age.

**Did you hear about the cop who moonlighted
as a comedian?
It didn't work out. He kept telling the audience
they had the right to remain silent.**

Did you hear about the DMV clerk who resigned
on Tuesday? He wanted to resign on Monday,
but he was standing in the wrong line.

**What did the Zen Buddhist say to the
pizza guy?
"Make me one with everything."**

Working in a bank sucks.
You're never allowed to take home free samples.

What do you call the owner of an
American-made car?
A pedestrian.

**Did you hear about the moron
gambler who lost $50 on one field
goal attempt?
He lost $25 on the field goal . . .
and $25 more on the instant replay.**

How do you know when a firing squad
really doesn't know what they're doing?
They're standing in a circle.

Did you hear about the guy
who swallowed goose feathers?
He felt a little down in the mouth.

Beverly Hills is so wealthy . . .
the Mercedes dealerships have
back-to-school sales.

**A horse walks into a bar. The
bartender looks at him and says,
"Hey, why the long face?"**

You know you have a bad landlord when
you tell him you have roaches and he
raises your rent for keeping pets.

**The good thing about inflation is that
it lets you live in more and more
expensive neighborhoods without
ever having to move.**

You know it's time to go to the dentist if no one tells you jokes because they're afraid you'll smile.

Say what you will about burglars . . .
just remember they're the only guys who
still make house calls.

Things sure are different today. Now when kids play Cowboys and Indians, the Indian kids don't shoot arrows . . .
they run casinos.

What's the only place in the world where
you can take a bath without water?
Wall Street.

Did you hear about the absent-minded mechanic who drowned?
He was out on a motorboat when the engine stalled, and he took a look underneath to see what was wrong.

A man says to his wife, "I'm going to the pub. Get your coat on."

His wife asks, "Does that mean you're taking me with you?"

"No, I'm turning off the heat."

A man tells his buddy, "I can't break my wife of the habit of staying up until five in the morning."

"What is she doing?" asks his buddy.

"Waiting for me to get home."

A guy starts chatting with a girl in a bar. "What's your name?" he asks.

"Carmen," she says. "I changed my name from Mary-Lou to Carmen because I love cars and men."

"I see," he says.

"What's your name?" she asks him.

He thought for a second. "Beersex."

What do you call 500 lawyers at the bottom of the ocean?
A good start.

Did you hear about the moron who refused the job of president of the United States? No chances for advancement.

A man walks up to a guy behind a counter and says, "Lemme have some grits and an RC cola."

The guy behind the counter looks at him and says, "You must be from Georgia."

Indignant, the man says, "What kind of stereotypical remark is that? If I ordered a sausage, would you think I was Polish?"

"No."

"If I asked for some chow mein, would you think I was Chinese?"

"No."

"Then why the hell would you think I'm from Georgia?"

"This is a hardware store."

Did you hear about the guy who was allergic to cotton? He had pills that would help. He just couldn't get them out of the bottle.

**Wouldn't it be great if you knew when
and where you were going to die?
Then you just don't show up.**

Women are so economical. Take birthday cakes.
They always make do with at least eight candles
fewer than they need.

**Life's greatest pleasures are the simple
ones.
Like seeing the car that cut you off three
miles back pulled over by the cops.**

You know what's great about baseball?
The pine tar, the resin, the grass, the dirt . . .
and that's just the hot dogs.

**Bank machines in Las Vegas are a little
different than anywhere else.
After you make a withdrawal, they ask if
you'd like to go double or nothing.**

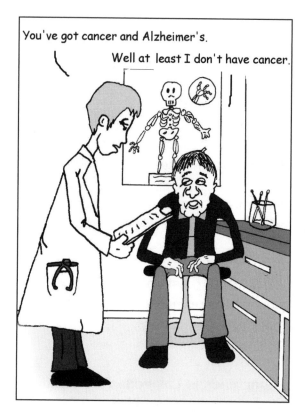

Scientists say that exercise kills germs.
Now if we can just figure out how to get
the damn things to exercise.

Here's a consumer tip.
Never eat at a restaurant where the
placemats have instructions for the
Heimlich maneuver.

The fat lady at the circus married the
India rubber man.
In three weeks, he erased her altogether.

Two five-year-old kids were looking
at an abstract painting in a museum.
Finally, one said, "Let's get out of
here before they say we did it."

Did you hear about the one-armed fisherman?
He had a terrible time telling how big the one that got away was.

One company has decided to put a picture of a hockey player on a can of soup, which makes sense.
It's probably the only thing you can eat without teeth.

After the bank had been robbed for the third time, the FBI agent asked the teller, "Did you notice anything special about the robber?"

"Yes," said the teller, "he was better dressed each time."

You know your wages have been frozen when you open your pay envelope and a light goes on.

Grandma and Grandpa are sitting at the breakfast table. Suddenly, Grandma gets up and slaps Grandpa on the head with a rolled-up newspaper.

"What was that for?" he asks her.

Grandma says, "That was for 40 years of bad sex."

Grandpa starts muttering, rolls up his newspaper, and slaps Grandma on the head.

"What's that for?" she asks.

"That's for knowing the difference."

Two men are fishing at a riverbank when a funeral procession drives by. One of the men stands up, takes off his hat, holds it over his heart, and bows.

"That was a nice thing to do," the other man tells him.

"Well, we were married for 25 years.

Why do men take showers instead of baths? Because pissing in the bathtub is disgusting.

The problem with unemployment
is that the minute you wake up in the
morning you're on the job.

One day Jesus came across an
adulteress crouching in a corner with
a crowd around her preparing to stone
her to death. Jesus stopped them and
said, "Let him who is without sin cast
the first stone."

Suddenly, a woman at the back of the
crowd fired off a stone at the adulteress.

Jesus glared at the woman and said,
"Mother, sometimes you really *tick me
off!*"

Pay phones are like government workers.
Only one in three actually works.

**Did you hear about the immigrant
who came to America seeking
freedom?
It didn't work out. His wife came over
on the next boat.**

Did you hear about the woman who
was such a clean freak?
She vacuumed so much the guy
downstairs went bald.

**Did you hear about the moron at
the fitness club?
He saw a sign that said "Free
Weights" . . .
so he took some.**

Why do gorillas have such big nostrils?
You ever seen the size of their fingers?

Did you hear about the dumb family that froze to
death outside a drive-in theater?
They were waiting to see the movie Closed for
the Winter.

Did you hear about the young boy whose
mother caught him masturbating and
warned him to stop because he'd go blind.
He asked if he could keep going just until
he needed glasses.

Before marriage, you take each other's breath
away.
After marriage, you suffocate each other.

If a person with multiple personalities
threatens suicide . . .
is that considered a hostage situation?

What's the definition of feedback?
The inevitable result when your baby doesn't appreciate strained carrots.

What does it mean when the flag is flying at half mast at the post office?
They're hiring.

If you're sending someone Styrofoam, what do you pack it in?

If vegetarians eat vegetables, what do humanitarians eat?

Did you hear about the cross-training woman who had her dead husband buried with his butt sticking out of the ground?
So she would have somewhere to park her bicycle.

An insurance broker gets a call from a woman.

"Can you insure a house over the phone?" she asks him.

"No, ma'am. I'd have to see it first."

"Well, you'd better get over here right away, because the place is on fire."

A guy has a date with Siamese twins. Later his friend asks him if he had a good time.
"Yes and no."

After examining the contents of the employee suggestion box, the boss complained, "I wish they'd be more specific. What kind of kite? Which lake?"

It's always bad luck when 13 people are drinking at the bar . . .
and you're paying the check.

Little Red Riding Hood is walking in the forest when she sees the Big Bad Wolf crouched down behind a log. "My, what big eyes you have, Mr. Wolf."

The surprised wolf jumps up and runs away.

Farther down the road, Little Red Riding Hood sees the wolf again. This time he's crouched behind a tree stump. "My, what big ears you have, Mr. Wolf," she says.

Again the wolf jumps up and runs away.

A few miles later, she sees the wolf yet again, only now he's crouched behind a road sign. "My, what big teeth you have, Mr. Wolf," taunts Little Red Riding Hood.

With that the wolf jumps up and snarls, "Will you get lost! I'm trying to take a dump."

What do you call a woman with one leg? Eileen.

What did one psychiatrist say to the other when they met on the street?
"You're fine, how am I?"